Parable of the
HURRICANE

by Herbert E. Douglass

Pacific Press Publishing Association
Mountain View, California
Oshawa, Ontario

Unless otherwise indicated, Bible quotations in this book are from the Revised Standard Version.

Cover photo from United Press International

Library of Congress Cataloging in Publication Data

Douglass, Herbert E
Parable of the hurricane.

   1. Second Advent. 2. Mississippi—Hurricane, 1969—Miscellanea. 3. Louisiana—Hurricane, 1969—Miscellanea. 4. Dominica—Hurricane, 1979—Miscellanea.
I. Title.
BT886.D69   232′.6   80-10712
ISBN 0-8163-0356-8

The Parable of the Hurricane

The kingdom of God is like unto those who hearken diligently to the warnings of the approaching hurricane, preparing their households for its coming fury. The hurricane buildeth in strength in seas afar. Its outstretched arms hurl bullets of rain at awesome speed. Its swirling winds are unmerciful.

Whence it cometh and whither it goeth is charted by satellite and measured by instruments precise; no one in its path needeth to be surprised.

But many are those who hearken but obey not. The wind cometh; their homes are not prepared; they are not ready—and the end of them is terrible indeed.

But they who take heed unto the warnings save both themselves and their households.

He who hath an ear let him hear the Parable of the Hurricane.

"One man met me at the door of a second-floor apartment with a drink in his hand. Must have been twenty people in there, and I asked them all to leave. Another told me that this was his land and if the sheriff wanted him to leave, he'd have to arrest him," relates Police Chief Jerry Peralta of Pass Christian, Mississippi, recalling that fateful evening of August 17, 1969.

"I told them that I couldn't order them out, but I could take from them the names of their next of kin. And that's when they laughed."

All day long Chief Peralta had sped up and down the highways, stopping at every home, urging everyone to leave immediately. For days a hurricane had been building in the Gulf of Mexico, its course and clout calculated as it gathered extraordinary strength in the warm seas. At nightfall, with the storm's winds blowing at sixty miles per hour and the breakers splashing over the seawall, Peralta had decided to make his last call on the hurricane party in the posh Richelieu apartments overlooking the beach.

A few hours after the chief left the party at the Richelieu, all the lights and electric power in Pass Christian went out in a single stroke. Fifteen minutes later, a giant wave, as high as a three-story house, slammed over the seawall, demolishing everything in its path.

The Richelieu apartments, steel and concrete, were overwhelmed by the rushing waters and torn to pieces by the ferocious winds. The whole building collapsed in a pile of rubble, killing the twenty people who had gathered for their cozy hurricane party. Twenty people ignored the radio warnings all day long and laughed at the sheriff's last call to flee for their lives.

That night the worst killer storm ever to hit North America had slammed into Mississippi and Louisiana. We called it Camille, and it blew harder than any hurricane ever recorded. It hurled bullets of rain at 210 miles per hour, killed 235 people in a single night, and smashed property worth well over a billion dollars.

Will we listen to the Parable of the Hurricane?

In the eastern Caribbean the weekend of August 25 and 26, 1979 was all that the tourist brochures could promise. Deep blue skies; brilliant sun; soft, warm breezes—all that a vacationer could want, punctuated only occasionally by refreshing rain showers. But it was hurricane season.

A thousand miles east of Barbados—the outrider of the chain of islands bordering the eastern Caribbean—a tropical storm was forming which was soon to be a vast whirlwind of enormous violence. This brewing storm, which we called David, was to become the Goliath of Caribbean hurricanes of this century.

Two of the most famous hurricane centers in the world, San Juan and Miami, went to work. On Monday, August 27, Miami advised the Caribbean that the Atlantic storm had become a hurricane: "David's position at noon [Monday] was 11.8 North and 51.5 West, some 600 miles east of Barbados. Moving westward at 15 to 20 miles per hour, its maximum estimated winds were 85 mph with gales (winds between 39 and 73 mph) extending 125 miles to the north of the hurricane's centre and 50 miles to the south of the centre."—*The Bajan and South Caribbean,* October 1979, p. 4.

All the Caribbean was put on "hurricane alert," while Barbados was issued a "hurricane warning." At 6:00 a.m. Tuesday, Miami advised that David had developed the potential of a killer, not seen in the Caribbean since Donna, in 1960: "David's position was 12.7 North and 55.3 West which placed it 300 miles east of Barbados. The highest sustained winds were calculated to be 130 mph with gale force winds 125 miles to the north of centre and 75 miles to the south of centre."—*Ibid*.

By now all ships had left Bridgetown, the chief harbor in Barbados, sailing south and away from hurricane danger.

At noontime Tuesday, San Juan reported "David's position to be 13.1 North and 56.7 West, 200 miles east of Barbados. Highest sustained winds . . . were about 150 mph extending 50 miles from centre in all directions with gale force winds 150 miles from centre in the northern semi-circle and 100 miles south of centre in the southern semi-circle."—*Ibid*.

San Juan went on to say that Hurricane David was developing into "the most intense to threaten the Windward Islands in this century and compares to the 1831 hurricane of Barbados and 1891 of Martinique." Of course few would be the people, if any, who could remember the ferocity of such earlier storms. For many the impending devastation was still unreal.

The flags with the red squares were hoisted everywhere. Barbados had battened down; Bridgetown had become a ghost city. But Barbados was spared the full fury of David as the reckless storm passed just north of the island by Tuesday midnight.

Wednesday morning at six "David's position was 14.5 North and 60.3 West, 35 miles east of Martinique, uncomfortably close to St. Lucia and moving towards Dominica."—*Ibid*. The angry sea, propelling tree trunks and debris as battering rams, scoured the beaches, rearranging them forever.

Eye Over Dominica

By 10:00 a.m., David's eye passed over Dominica, and the island will never again be the same. Eyewitnesses compare southern Dominica to the Hiroshima of August 6, 1945—a brown, bare, destroyed landscape.

Out of a population of 81,000, approximately 60,000 were homeless, with thirty-seven known dead. More than 90 percent of the island's electrical power had been supplied by hydroelectric plants; they now lay shattered with ruptured flumes. All electric poles were reported down; restoring electric service would cost an estimated $15,000,000. Losses from agriculture, the island's main industry, were staggering: bananas, 95 percent; grapefruit, 75 percent; coconuts, 75 percent; limes, 65 percent; other crops, 80 percent; forestry reserves, 70 to 80 percent.

Not for nothing did the Indians of the Guianas call these tropical storms *hyacoran,* or devil; the Haitian Indians used the word *huracan,* meaning evil spirit.

But was the loss of life on Dominica necessary? The appalling fact was that while the whole world for days apprehensively followed the track of this "storm of the century," "the only people who did not seem to be worrying about David were those towards whom it was heading."—*Ibid.*

Precautions on Dominica seemed to be nonexistent. The first indication of this lethargy came three days after the storm had struck. A leading spokesman for the Caribbean Development Bank, who was a resident of Dominica, appeared on Barbados TV to give his account of David's fury. To the astonishment of his audience, he complained that Dominica had not been given enough warning. "Only four hours," he said. He spoke for many others who also found their way to Barbados.

One observer wrote, "The immediate reaction of many viewers was to wonder if Dominicans were living in the same world." After all, neighboring islands had been seeing and hearing about David for at least five days.

9

The same radio broadcasts and TV programs heard and seen by the Barbadians were beamed to Dominica. But somehow Dominicans seemed oblivious to the stationary satellite that hovered over the Caribbean for the sole purpose of giving that area accurate information about weather changes. The precision information radioed back from the brave pilots of the American reconnaissance aircraft that flew into the eye of David was relayed to Dominica. The continuing drop of the atmospheric pressure, which was 27.52 inches at Tuesday noon, should have been warning enough.

During this same period Barbadians feverishly erected storm shutters and nailed up their homes. Business on the island had shut down except for the radio station, which continued to give out the latest information, noting the increasing enormity of the danger.

While all this went on in Barbados, Dominica was declaring itself to be only on "hurricane watch." One Dominican lady interviewed later recalled "that they regarded all this as just another instance of the false alarms they had been given year after year. They were fed up, she said, with rushing to buy food and lanterns at the last minute and then all the paraphernalia of battening down and retiring to their storm cellars, all for nothing."—*Ibid.*, p. 3.

Dominica, unlike its sister islands, was not even on "hurricane alert" on Tuesday evening! "In one of the most irresponsible acts of any public service during a national emergency, Radio Dominica went off the air at their scheduled time of 10:00 p.m. Consequently, when at 10:45 on Tuesday night the Barbados Met Office informed their counterparts that David had not only missed Barbados but was then . . . moving dead-on for Dominica, there was no way of informing the Dominican public other than the ancient warning system of ringing the church bells. But even this system seems to have become outmoded in Dominica."—*Ibid*.

Like a Thief in the Night

Not until 10:45 a.m. Wednesday was Barbados able to make contact with officialdom in Dominica—only to be told by the Minister of Communication that "the weather had been fine up to eight o'clock that morning and everybody had gone to work as usual. He did however notice that the sky was then overcast and strong winds were already blowing, but it was probably blowing stronger in Martinique. Like a thief in the night, David had crept up on them, and Dominicans had opened their doors in the morning to let him in."—*Ibid*.

They refused to be warned. They did not "know" because they refused to hear.

Will we learn the lesson of the Parable of the Hurricane?

Another storm, greater than Camille or David, is soon to break over planet Earth. The Bible calls it the seven last plagues, Armageddon, "a time of trouble, such as never has been since there was a nation till that time." Daniel 12:1.

But before this storm breaks, God will have given a worldwide message to prepare for the worst. No one will ever look back and say that he never heard the warning. Do you know what that message says?

Jesus likened this coming storm and warning message to the days of Noah. When we talk about the storm in Noah's day, we are talking about a big-league storm—a storm so big, so global, so final that the whole world was flooded and no one survived except those who responded to God's warning message. See Genesis 6 to 8. There is something very final about laughing at one's last warning to prepare for the coming storm.

In Matthew 24 Jesus says, "As were the days

of Noah, so will be the coming of the Son of man. For as in those days before the flood they were eating and drinking, marrying and giving in marraige, until the day when Noah entered the ark, and they did not know until the flood came and swept them all away, so will be the coming of the Son of man." Verses 37-39.

What could Jesus mean—"*they* did not *know*"? After all, Noah had been warning his world for 120 years. What kind of message was it that Noah preached? And what kind of man was Noah that God could entrust to him such an important assignment?

Noah was a prototype of people who listen to God in these last days. We read in Genesis 6:9, "Noah was a righteous man, blameless in his generation; Noah walked with God."

Emphasis on Righteousness

His message was clear and uncompromising. Peter tells us that Noah was a "preacher of righteousness." 2 Peter 2:5, K.J.V.

Why was this emphasis on righteousness so important? Take a look at Noah's world, a world that had lost its grip on morality and fidelity—where righteousness was almost extinguished.

The record states that "the Lord saw that

the wickedness of man was great in the earth, and that every imagination of the thoughts of his heart was only evil continually." "And God saw the earth, and behold, it was corrupt; for all flesh had corrupted their way upon the earth." Genesis 6:5, 12.

No wonder Noah preached a message of righteousness. He wasn't about to give Band-Aids of sweet talk and religious comfort when a storm was ready to break. He went to the heart of the problem. His world needed more than education and a government plan to redistribute wealth, more than increased leisure and less work. He called for a change in life-style. He called on his neighbors to listen to the mercy offered by their Creator—to obey and conform to His likeness. As he looked around, it was obvious that a pattern of life contrary to righteousness leads to a life-style so corrupt that "every imagination of the thoughts [is] . . . evil continually." Then, as now, no ground existed for moral neutrality.

"As were the days of Noah, so will be the coming of the Son of man." Let us listen to what Jesus is saying. At the end of time God's message will again be emphatically a call to righteousness; an appeal to accept God's pardon and power in order to live "blameless" lives in our generation, even as Noah did in His. Jesus knew that without blameless lives His followers would have little credibility when they spoke for God as Noah did in his generation.

Before the end of time, in the last days preceding judgment, there will be people who, like Noah, will respond to the call for righteousness—a "call for the endurance of the saints, those who keep the commandments of God and the faith of Jesus." Revelation 14:12. More about this later.

But what will world conditions be like during those last days? One of our clues is "As were the days of Noah." Noah preached his message of righteous living by faith at a time when "the earth was corrupt in God's sight, and . . . filled with violence." Genesis 6:11.

Do we really need to elaborate on the comparison between Noah's day and ours? But some observations seem to be in order. First, it is more than interesting to observe that a violent, morally decadent society in Noah's day was not sufficient evidence, not a persuasive argument, that the end was at hand. Men and women are not frightened for long by the so-called breakdown of society.

Strange but true—fear is not a lasting emotion. It is a highly effective and persuasive technique used by demagogues, shortsighted parents, politicians, and preachers to get immediate results. But impulsive decisions do not last. Nothing is really changed.

Fear is a negative emotion that temporarily stops a particular action, but fear cannot be relied upon to induce a positive change. God, through His prophets in all ages, has presented fearful alternatives as He has appealed to people to consider their ways. But His main emphasis has been the positive appeal, fleshed out with love and grace. For this reason, persuasive techniques that appeal primarily to a fear response—such as appealing to others on the basis of judgments to come: that hellfire awaits them, that the world cannot last another ten years because of its pollution, population, and natural resource problems—are doomed to fail if a positive, changed life-style is the desired result.

Easy to Baptize the Fearful

Although many were moved temporarily by fear, Noah's hearers would not truly repent and live righteous lives by faith in their Creator. Furthermore, God did not want merely fearful people in the ark; He knows that only those committed to keep His commandments and live by faith in His promises of pardon and power are truly safe to save. It is easy to baptize the fearful; it is another matter to build up the church with those who will endure unto the end, committed to His commandments and motivated by the faith of Jesus.

Our second observation follows: Noah's generation "did not know." Matthew 24:39. What did they not know? They thought they knew much. They "knew," on the basis of anything that could be seen or heard, that there was no reason to expect doom. True, the world was a mess, society was in constant upheaval, and strife was common. Just like many old-timers who had already seen hurricanes, before Camille struck Mississippi and Louisiana or before David slammed into Dominica, Noah's contemporaries were used to periodic troubles. Furthermore, many were emotionally anesthetized with the thought "It can't happen to me."

But what's new? Entire generations of people can get used to tensions, temporary solutions, and changing life-styles. We muddle through somehow, and our fears are soon forgotten. For Noah's generation the future looked bright. After all, the professors, religious leaders, and scientists told them it would be!

Apply our second observation to the end of the world: When the door of probation closes on this world—just as surely as the door of Noah's ark was closed by the angel while the sky was still blue—it will look safe enough, based on anything that can be seen or heard, to last for generations to come. Satan will make sure of that!

Peter, under divine inspiration, reminds us that "scoffers will come in the last days with scoffing, following their own passions and saying, 'Where is the promise of his coming?' " 2 Peter 3:3, 4.

All this suggests that those concerned exclusively with pessimistic predictions regarding the state of the world before the close of probation will be disappointed and will probably be just as lost as those who scoffed at Noah.

A gifted religious writer joins Peter in noting: "Come when it may, the day of God will come unawares to the ungodly. When life is going on in its unvarying round; when men are absorbed in pleasure, in business, in traffic, in money-making; when religious leaders are magnifying the world's progress and enlightenment, and the people are lulled in a false security—then, as the midnight thief steals within the unguarded dwelling, so shall sudden destruction come upon the careless and ungodly 'and they shall not escape.' "—Ellen White, *The Great Controversy*, p. 38.

"Christ declares that there will exist . . . unbelief concerning His second coming. . . . When the professed people of God are uniting with the world, living as they live, and joining with them in forbidden pleasures; when the luxury of the world becomes the luxury of the church; when the marriage bells are chiming, and all are looking forward to many years of worldly prosperity—then, suddenly as the lightning flashes from the heavens, will come the end of their bright visions and delusive hopes."—*Ibid.*, pp. 338, 339.

"The crisis is stealing gradually upon us. The sun shines in the heavens, passing over its usual round, and the heavens still declare the glory of God. Men are still eating and drinking, planting and building, marrying and giving in marriage. Merchants are still buying and selling. Men are jostling one against another, contending for the highest place. Pleasure lovers are still crowding to theaters, horse races, gambling hells. The highest excitement prevails, yet probation's hour is fast closing, and every case is about to be eternally decided. Satan sees that his time is short. He has set all his agencies at work that men may be deceived, deluded, occupied and entranced, until the day of probation shall be ended, and the door of mercy be forever shut."—Ellen White, *The Desire of Ages*, p. 636.

The Close of Probation

In other words, those unprepared for the close of probation that will occur a short time before Jesus returns will not "know" the truth about transpiring events, because they refuse to know. Apparently they prefer to "know" what best supports their personal desires and selfish ambitions. They "know" only what coincides with their presuppositions.

All this leads us to a third observation: It seems that world conditions prior to the close of probation will give the last generation no more direct, indisputable warning than world conditions, prior to the Flood, gave to Noah's hearers.

How can this be? It's the dilemma of a recent cartoon: Two men were observing two other men, each of whom was carrying a sign. One sign read, "The world is about to end!" The other, "The world will never end!" One of the bystanders said to the other, "One's a pessimist and the other's an optimist. But I'm not sure which is which!"

Our modern dilemma! For every expert who forecasts the doom of planet Earth, there is another—equally trained academically and technologically—who argues convincingly that the future never looked brighter!

It's the paradox of horror—repeated doses of outrage and horror inoculate one into insensitivity. We learn from inspired writers that world conditions *prior* to the unprecedented time of trouble (the period of the seven last plagues when even the imaginations of science-fiction writers will be surpassed by reality) may not seem sufficiently dreadful to cause the world's billions to hasten to repentance.

After living through decades of unprecedented global horror, after teetering for years on the brink of nuclear disaster, numb with statistics describing millions living on a starvation level or plagued by pollution disasters—more of the same only seems to anesthetize further our sensibilities. We find ourselves turning the pages of newspapers or magazines, each full of incredible disaster somewhere, as if horror is as normal as the weather report.

The truth is that prospects of a peaceful, pleasant world may be more promising and believable for those living just before the close of probation than at any other time in world history. If the world appears on the verge of removing dreadful physical diseases, pollution problems, hunger, and poverty, as well as establishing an unprecedented world peace federation, will not dire warnings of the end of the world seem as unreal and unbelievable as the words of lonely Noah as he implored his neighbors to enter the ark?

The same open disdain, ridicule, and general unconcern which met Noah's message of doom will be duplicated as time runs out in the days immediately before the close of probationary time. Undisturbed by the routine litany of the world's ills, and afflicted with the numbness generated by a half-century cycle of seething tensions and intermittent relief, emotionally drained men and women may think of good reasons to discount or even write off the warnings of Seventh-day Adventists and others.

No question about it—troubles will be rampant and electronically presented before most families on all continents in living color on the 6:00 p.m. news. As time goes on—and with more people—troubles can be expected on an increasingly greater scale. But mankind has developed an enormous capacity to adjust to such troubles. Furthermore, in spite of it all, men and women seem profoundly eager to believe that technology will unfailingly come up with whatever is necessary to eventually wipe out all such causes for anxiety.

Many Reasons to Hope

In the midst of troubles and tensions, men and women will have much to stimulate their hopes and comfort their fears. Books for both the sophisticated and the common mind, television programs, seminars, and university classes—all are reminding us of the giant leaps of technology in solving world problems, especially in the last twenty-five years. Problems that seemed formidable only a quarter century ago are forgotten as if they never existed—or remembered only as relics of long-ago medieval times. Think of what the transistor and microelectronics have done for almost every industry. Or the Salk vaccine, CAT bodyscanners, Teflon, lasers, and polymers.

And according to many experts we can look forward to food supplies harvested through aquaculture rather than agriculture; weather manipulation and precise prediction; frozen embryos guaranteed free of birth defects and with all characteristics—color of hair and eyes, size, IQ, and sex—available for prospective parents to order; genetic therapy, utilizing appropriate dosages of DNA to remove all tendencies of allergy, obesity, arthritis, and cancer; artificial organs and parts for any section of the human body; improved healing via mind control and endorphins; safe, clean inexhaustible laser fusion solving a large percentage of world energy problems; and high-strength structural materials and super-duty fabrics—and the list is truly endless.

No wonder Ellen White warned that probation will close "when religious leaders are magnifying the world's progress and enlightenment," when "all are looking forward to many years of worldly prosperity."—*The Great Controversy*, pp. 38, 338.

No small wonder that Satan will so arrange matters that this world, amidst its "normal" tensions and moral decadence, will be "deceived, deluded, occupied and entranced" regarding the truth of impending judgment.—Ellen White, *The Desire of Ages*, p. 636. He will not play into God's hands by permitting society to fall apart drastically or by manipulating the forces of nature so that this planet is a denuded wasteland any more than he did in Noah's day prior to the end of the pre-Flood world. He will deceive, delude, and entrance so that whatever is intrinsically bad about this planet is balanced off with plausible, enthralling prospects of a world emerging from its growing pains. "As were the days of Noah."

Pessimists As Wrong As the Optimists

One of the chief purposes of the Seventh-day Adventist Church is to tell the truth about the future. We believe, going back to our cartoon, that the Bible makes it clear that the pessimists are wrong—the future is not hopeless. The world will not end in either a whimper or a bang. World nuclear powers will not incinerate the earth; we will not drown or be suffocated in our own garbage or shrivel up in mass starvation.

And the Bible makes it clear that the optimists are wrong—the future is not in the hands of ingenious men who, up to now, have always come up with the necessary solutions. Technology will not cure, for example, the self-interest of relatives or neighbors or nations, as they grab for what they have not earned, trampling all others in their path. Technology may recycle discarded glass and metals, but not the rising tide of moral garbage that mocks the rising standards of living everywhere.

What indeed could be more suffocating than a disease-free world, filled with homes for all and with adequate food guaranteed for every man, woman, and child (all very common and accepted expectations)—if that world wallows in its comforts and scorns the time-honored values of respect for property rights, fidelity to marital and moral commitments, honesty, purity, and industry?

In summary, Seventh-day Adventists are destined to tell the truth about the future, to proclaim the gospel loud and clear, and to say what God has on His mind regarding how this world will end. Their mission is strikingly similar to that of Noah's prior to the Flood. In fact, the kind of world in which Adventists are to proclaim their message is also strikingly similar to that of Noah's day, as Jesus made clear in Matthew 24:37 to 39.

Strange as it may seem today, those who died in the Flood thought that their civilization would go on forever. World conditions did not compel Noah's neighbors to listen to him as if they were listening to their last warning. Much to the contrary! Likewise, world conditions in the last days will not become so hopeless, so gloomy, that thoughtful people are compelled to run to the Adventist Church for fear of what is about to happen. "As were the days of Noah, so will be the coming of the Son of man."

Perhaps Satan's most sly and sinister plan will not be cloaked in the fear engendered by the pessimists but will instead be wrapped in the hope and explanations inspired by worldly optimists. The air of optimism finally choked those who laughed at Noah.

But "as were the days of Noah, so will be the coming of the Son of man." Those who are lost, unprepared for the seven last plagues (Revelation 16), religious perhaps but not committed, will be looking for "signs" other than the preaching of righteousness and the invitation of the Spirit to join those who "keep the commandments of God and the faith of Jesus." Revelation 14:12. They "will not know" when the door is shut, because they refuse "to know." What a pity!

Those who refused "to know" did not learn the Parable of the Hurricane. They spurned the only invitation by which they might be spared the awful storm of the last days. Do you know what that warning message says?

An Ominous Message

The most ominous message ever to be heard on planet Earth since Noah's day is recorded in Revelation 14. When it is clear that no more will respond—when its warning can do no more good—the storm breaks, a short while before Jesus returns. How one relates to this message will determine whether the coming of Jesus is good news or horrible news.

The story of this last warning message in the book of Revelation describes terrible things happening to those who ignore or reject this message—such consequences as "the wrath of God" (Revelation 14:10; 15:1; 16:1) and "the lake of fire" (Revelation 20:14).

But it also states that wonderful things happen to those who accept these messages of the three angels of Revelation 14:6 to 14. They are called God's people (Revelation 18:4); they are invited "to the marriage supper of the Lamb" (Revelation 19:9); God "will wipe away every tear from their eyes, and death shall be no more, neither shall there be mourning nor crying nor pain any more" (Revelation 21:4).

One thing is certain. We won't be able to pick and choose which messages we want or don't want. No alternatives. No substitutes. No waiting for another, easier message. This is it—this everlasting gospel of Revelation 14:6 to 12. Literally, there is nothing more that God can say or do for people on Planet Earth. In these last messages He is saying it all and can say no more, just as there came a time when Noah could say no more.

Every one of us owes it to himself and his loved ones to listen carefully to these warnings of mercy. Our future truly stands or falls on what we do with them. It *does* matter what we believe. We are not only what we eat, we are also what we think.

In these few pages we have not attempted to examine these three warning messages of Revelation 14. Other books have done it well. But a quick look at the first angel's message will emphasize the seriousness of this last warning before the storm.

The first angel's message creates the setting for all three. These messages are urgent, universal, everlasting, and expect a response. They proclaim the everlasting gospel, the consistent word from God heard from Genesis to Revelation. Their messages are urgent because they are the last warning before the storm, the siren signaling the approaching tornado, the appeal of a parent on the doorstep to a teenager bent on destroying himself. "Fear God and give him glory, for the hour of his judgment has come." Revelation 14:7.

The messages are universal because they will be heard by "every nation and tribe and tongue and people." Revelation 14:6. No one will be engulfed by the seven last plagues before he has been given the chance to avoid them.

Such messages produce results. At a time when dozens of false gospels are captivating the multitudes, the faithful preaching of the everlasting gospel will produce "those who keep the commandments of God and the faith of Jesus." Revelation 14:12.

That is why the three angels of Revelation 14 signal the last act in the drama of salvation. Faithful preaching of the everlasting gospel will hasten the moment when everyone living will have chosen to respond Yes or No to the gifts and claims of the everlasting gospel. Faithful preaching of the gospel will hasten the close of probation and the return of Jesus—and the end of the mounting horrors of a planet awash in misery, dashed hopes, and untold suffering.

John the revelator saw it clearly: the everlasting gospel produces commandment-keeping people who have the faith of Jesus. What our Lord's faith did for Him it will do for all His followers. The faith of Jesus produces the character of Jesus. Just as Jesus blended submissive obedience and His Father's enabling grace—so His loyal followers may. And nevermore so than in these last days, in response to His invitation and to His warning of the storm such as never was.

Those who "keep the commandments of God and the faith of Jesus" have responded to the "call for the endurance of the saints." Revelation 14:12. They have permitted Jesus to do His work of being man's Saviour. See Matthew 1:21. He has demonstrated before all the universe that He has the power to save mankind from the power of sin as well as its penalty. He will have proved that such people are truly the friendliest, healthiest, most trustworthy people on earth. And the most responsive to warnings of the impending storm. They will have learned well the Parable of the Hurricane. Have you?

If you want to read more about the subjects discussed in this book, write and request a list of books from the publisher:

Pacific Press Publishing Association
1350 Villa Street
Mountain View, California 94042